A Walk in the Fields

WALLACE KIRKLAND

REILLY & LEE BOOKS • CHICAGO

OTHER BOOKS IN THE SERIES:

A Walk by the Pond
A Walk in the Woods

I wish to thank Del Baston for his encouragement
and his help in filling gaps in my photography files.

Wallace Kirkland

To Parents and Teachers

My interest in field life began years ago, when I was covering buffalo on assignment for *Life* magazine. There were days when the buffalo hid far back in the hill country, and we didn't see any at all. But even on those occasions my time was not wasted. I spent many hours wandering through the fields, photographing what I found there. I have been studying field life and adding to my photographic collection ever since.

A field is a self-contained community that teems with life —even during the winter, when it is blanketed in snow. And, of course, the life of the field follows the seasons. It awakens and renews itself in spring and early summer and comes to fruition in late summer and fall.

I hope that this book will serve to awaken in my readers a sense of wonder—at the diversity of life that is found in the fields and the harmonious interdependence among all its plants and animals.

Wallace Kirkland

Any wide expanse of land that is free of buildings can be called a field. There are many kinds of fields—playing fields, battlefields, fields of corn and wheat, cotton and hay. These sheep are grazing in a grassy field, or "pasture," that has been set aside for them by a farmer. But the wild fields, the ones that have never been disturbed by man, are the most interesting of all. In them you can see all sorts of animal, plant, and insect life.

Prairie dogs live in the vast fields, or "plains," of the Midwest and West. These animals are about a foot long and are covered with coarse, gray brown hair. They have small, beady eyes and short tails. Prairie dogs live in groups, or "colonies." Their underground homes are called "burrows." To construct a burrow, the prairie dogs first dig a hole straight down, twelve feet deep or more. Then they dig a long, horizontal passageway, to which smaller "rooms" are connected. The burrow slopes up to a back exit. Prairie dogs build mounds of dirt around the burrow entrances to keep water out when there is heavy rain.

Cottontail rabbits dig their shallow nests in the fields. The mother lines her nest with grass or fur to keep her babies warm. Rabbits have very good eyesight, but they recognize other rabbits by smell. That is why rabbits' noses twitch all the time.

The striped ground squirrel, or chipmunk, is another animal
that you can find in the open fields. Like the prairie dog,
it lives underground. Ground squirrels eat nuts, roots, and
certain insects, and they often raid farmers' cornfields for food!
Ground squirrels have roomy pouches in their cheeks, which
they use to carry food back to their burrows for the winter.
During the cold months, ground squirrels spend most
of their time sleeping.

While ground squirrels and certain other field animals prefer to sleep away the winter, otters often leave their homes along the banks of lakes and streams to play "follow the leader" or toboggan in the open fields of snow. Their beautiful fur coats protect them from the cold.

As the snow melts and spring turns into summer, wild fields shimmer with colorful flowering plants. Tall prairie phlox appears by June. Its leaves grow in pairs all the way up the stem to a cluster of flowers at the top. The blossoms are white, pinkish, or purple.

Daisies, with their bright yellow centers and many white petals, are a common field flower.

Bellwort belongs to the lily family. Its flowers are yellow and bell-shaped, and they dangle from the top of the stem.

Lupine has white, yellow, and blue blossoms that look much like the flowers of the sweet pea. Many blooms grow on a single stem. The leaves of the lupine are star-like, with eight points.

Wild leek has a cluster of delicate white flowers nodding on a long, slender stem. The plant has a strong onion smell. The milk of cows that have fed on wild leek has an onion taste.

The fruit of the wild straw-
berry plant grows on trailing
vines. It is not a real berry,
however, because it has no
seed, or "pit," in the center.
As you can see, its seeds are
on the outside of the fruit,
instead. Wild strawberries are
smaller than the ones you
buy in the grocery store, but
they are very sweet and
good to eat.

The crab apple is a low,
bushy tree with reddish brown
bark. Because it needs a lot of
sun, it does not grow well in
thick forests. But it is often
found on the edges of fields.
In May and June it is covered
with sweet-smelling blos-
soms, pinkish white or deep
rose-colored. After the
blossoms have fallen, the tree
produces berries that are like
tiny sour apples. These crab
apples make very good jelly.

On your walk through the fields, you should be on the watch for two plants—poison ivy and bittersweet nightshade. Poison ivy grows in two ways: as a shrub about five feet high, and as a vine that attaches itself to tree trunks at the edges of fields.

The leaves are dark green and always grow in threes. The plant is poisonous to the touch, and it produces an itchy, painful rash that can spread quickly over your whole body.

Bittersweet nightshade grows on a vine. It has purple flowers with yellow centers. It produces green, egg-shaped berries, which turn first to yellow and then to red. The berries are beautiful to look at but poisonous to eat.

Certain weeds, such as dande-
lions, are unwelcome on lawns,
because their long roots choke
out the grasses and are hard to
pull out. But many weeds grow
freely in wild fields, and some of
them are quite pretty.

Queen Ann's lace, above,
covers the field with a snowy
white quilt. It is really a wild
carrot, but its roots are shorter
than the farmer's carrot and not
very good to eat.

Fleabane, with its small, rose
violet flowers, is a common weed.
People used to think it would
drive fleas away, and that is how
fleabane got its name. The plant
contains an oil that is used in
making mosquito repellent.

The beautiful yellow flower of the goldenrod appears late in the summer in many fields. As you can see, there are many shoots of flowers on a single stalk. The goldenrod is the state flower of Kansas, Nebraska, and Alabama.

The Canada thistle is another late-blooming weed. Its flowers are purplish, and its leaves are spiny. Farmers dislike the Canada thistle because it spreads very quickly and chokes out their crops. It is against the law in many states to allow the seeds to mature.

You can find clumps of milkweed blooming in August. If you break off a leaf, a milky sap oozes out, and that is how the plant got its name.

After the milkweed blooms, pods form. Each pod is filled with many seeds. Each seed has hundreds of hairs that are packed close together, like a folded umbrella. When the seeds are ripe, the pod springs open, and the seeds float away on the air. They are very light. The U.S. Navy once used milkweed seeds to fill life preservers.

Of course, the many plants in wild fields attract lots of insect life. The monarch butterfly, for example, lays its eggs on the milkweed. The monarch spends the winter in California and parts of Mexico. In the spring it comes to the northern states, where milkweed grows. It lays its eggs on the underside of the milkweed leaf. The eggs hatch into caterpillars that feed on the milkweed leaves. At the end of the summer, each caterpillar attaches itself to a leaf and forms a cocoon. Inside the cocoon, it changes into a monarch butterfly. Then, before frost comes, the monarch joins hundreds of other butterflies. They fly back, or "migrate," to the area from which their parents came, and there they spend the winter.

Aphids are often called plant lice. Their mouths are shaped
for sucking the juices from plants, and aphids are very harmful to plant life. As aphids eat, they discharge a sweet juice,
which ants like to feed on.

Ladybird beetles are the aphids' worst enemies. The ladybirds eat aphids in huge numbers, and the beetles are in great demand by orange grove owners to keep the aphids under control.

Locusts, like aphids, are very harmful to plants. There
are many kinds of locusts, but all of them feed on
roots, leaves, or other plant parts. Locusts band
together in huge, hungry swarms. If there are enough
of them, they can destroy acres of plant life in just
a few meals.

The red-banded leafhopper is a tremendous jumper. It sucks the sap from such plants as goldenrod and clover. Like aphids, the leafhoppers produce a sweet juice, or "honey-dew," as they feed, which attracts ants and bees.

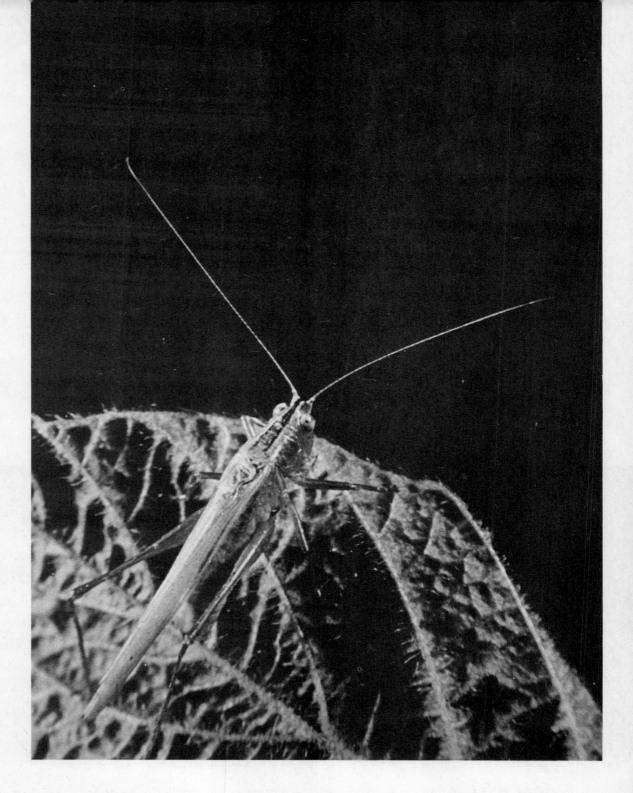

The long-horned grasshopper is related to certain locusts and the red-banded leafhopper. It is named for its antennae, which are much longer than its body. The antennae are mostly for smelling, but also for touching. The grasshopper jumps from one plant to another, looking for tender green leaves and stems to eat. When a grasshopper is in danger and frightened, it spits out a brown liquid.

The spittle bug is a curious, beetle-like insect. The mother makes a froth on the stems of plants and grasses to cover her eggs. The young spittle bug also covers itself with froth while it feeds. The froth looks like spittle, and that is how the insect got its name.

On your walk in the fields you are very likely to see a honey-
bee. As many as 30,000 honeybees can be found in a single
nest, or "hive." Most of these bees are female "workers."
They gather the sweet juices, called "nectar," from the
flowering plants and make it into honey. The workers have
other jobs, too. They build the hive and add new rooms, or
"cells," as they are needed to store honey and eggs. The
workers also keep the hive clean and protect it from enemies.

Each hive has only one queen bee, such as the one you can see here emerging from a special queen cell. Young female bees who will develop into queens are fed a food called "royal jelly." The first queen to emerge from her cell breaks into the other queen cells and stings the unborn queens to death.

   Every hive also has a number of male bees, or "drones." The drones never do any work, and they have to be fed by the worker bees. One of the drones mates with the queen as she flies in the air, and the queen spends the rest of her life laying eggs. When the summer is over, the workers throw the drones out of the hive. The drones are unable to take care of themselves, and they die.

The mud dauber wasp uses mud to build a number of long tubes side by side, without the help of workers. Its nest looks like a set of organ pipes. Each tube is divided into several small cells. The mother wasp catches a number of spiders and injects them with a fluid that paralyzes but does not kill them. She stores the spiders in a cell, then deposits an egg in the cell and seals it off.

Although the adult wasp lives on plant juices, the young wasp, or "larva," needs fresh, live food. After the egg hatches, the larva feeds on the spiders that its mother stocked in the cell. It emerges from the cell as a fully grown adult.

The cliff swallow, like the mud
dauber wasp, builds its nest of
mud. Low areas in a field some-
times become very muddy after a
heavy rainfall. The swallows seek
out these spots and scoop up
mud by the beakful, often
carrying it to a barn on a nearby
farm. Cliff swallows build their
jug-shaped nests in groups. The
nests are lined with feathers
and grass.

Whenever English sparrows come upon a cluster of swallow nests, the sparrows will form in groups to drive the swallows away. The sparrows break the swallow eggs or push the young swallows out of the nest. Then the sparrows move in and lay their own eggs. Sparrows feed on seeds, for the most part, and they are very useful for controlling the spread of weeds.

Try to find an open field in the area where you live. You might ask a grownup to help you identify all the plants, animals, and insects that you see. As the seasons change, there is much in every field to learn about and enjoy—if only you will take the time to look for it.